Anxiety is a Habit

Daily chunks of thought to train your mind to overcome anxiety

Sophie Kemp Cathcart

There was a point in which anxiety controlled my life. I didn't see a way out - it was so terrifyingly strong and all-consuming that I had submitted to the fact that it is something I would just always live with. It wasn't going to go away, so my goal became finding ways to cope and deal with it - ways to make every day at least a little bearable.

I was wrong. SO wrong. Anxiety is not a "thing" that you catch and get stuck with. No matter how much it may feel so, it is not a constant in your life - never has been, never will be. Anxiety is a temporary reaction to negative external events, and it is this realisation that flicked a switch in my head.

And the more I started to invest in this realisation, the more the epiphanies that make up this book came.

Having been in the depths of the wrath of anxiety though, I know first-hand how hard it can be to sit still for more than 5 minutes and focus on a task. That's why, rather than one long, continuous (and daunting) prose, this book takes the structure of small chunks of thought; short, digestible perspectives and ideas to consider daily. Don't rush through the book. Instead, read one idea a day, and through the rest of that day, explore the idea deeply, apply it to your own life, talk about it with others, and you will gradually train your mind into a mindset capable of eradicating anxiety from your life once and for all.

Note: this book was written during the Covid-19 pandemic, and this is often referred to, however, its teachings and ideas indefinitely extend into post-pandemic times... whatever they may look like!

Acknowledgements

I can't ever thank my parents enough for all of their support in getting me through the worst time of my life - I really do owe them the world. The same goes for all my family and close friends (you know who you are) who have kept me going through everything.

But the person that this book wouldn't exist without is my boyfriend. The first person who every really "got" me. Thank you for the endless amounts of time, energy and compassion you have given me. It's pretty crazy just how much you have helped me in such a short space of time.

I love you all.

To anyone and everyone who finds themselves under the wrath of anxiety.

You've got this.

Backstory

There are two key things which helped me in overcoming anxiety:

a) Changes in perspective

b) The gym

A little background. *After contracting a viral infection which lasted over a year in 2014, my weight dropped to scarily low weight. More so than the weight loss though, what was the most scarring thing about this was the anxiety it led to. Once diagnosed (it took a while as the virus often lay dormant), the virus was treated easily enough, but the resulting anxiety was anything but that. It totally and utterly consumed me.*

*Before all of this, I had been a straight grade, super high achiever who fully believed in the ability of my own brain. Fast forward to post illness though, and I genuinely believed I had lost **all** of this. I 100% believed that anxiety was in control - that it was THAT powerful - and always would be. I didn't believe in being able to change your own thoughts and mental identity (or maybe I did deep down, but the anxiety overrode any chance it had). My mind was strong, but the anxiety was stronger. Through first and second year university I did alright, but achieved nothing like the grades I was used to.*

What did help me back then though, was exercise. Somehow, despite such a low weight (which the anxiety made extremely hard to fix) and physical trauma, my body allowed me to continue to work out. Note - I realise that this probably wasn't technically the best idea, but I was so desperately in need of some sort of escape from my own head. BUT, back then, for some reason, I attributed this solely to the fact that my body was a machine and did not require brain power to work well. As I saw it then, my brain had been destroyed, but the exercise could keep me stable enough to get by despite this. I remember only a few weeks after recovering from the virus, I ran a 5k race. Looking at me, you would have thought it impossible, but somehow, my "machine" of a body got me through, and I won the race over hundreds.

I can't remember specifically the point that everything changed, but what I do know is that I have the gym to thank for it. Through meeting lots of like-minded people, my mind started to open, and my perspective began to shift. The strength realised through witnessing my own body continue to grow in strength despite such past trauma began to translate to the obvious strength my mind clearly still held, and that's when it really clicked.

My "machine" body had achieved **nothing** independent of the brain which I had thought to become so useless. It was my mind that told my body how to recover and rebuild physically, how to push through barriers workout wise, how to reach my goal of the 5k. And if my mind could control the recovery of my body following such trauma (with no conscious thought at that), there was no reason at all that it couldn't do the same for its own mentality (especially if I committed to it with conscious intent). The problem was, I had given anxiety total control, and as a result, my mental health depended totally on external factors. BUT, through realising my own strength (proven to me through my physical gym-aided recovery), I *became attuned to the fact that internal control, in which what happens around you doesn't control your head, is 100% achievable given enough self-care, time, and commitment. My previous dismissive opinion of re-training your brain and its thoughts towards bettering your wellbeing was totally turned on its head.*

*And with that shift in mindset, my "old" brain resurged (we will return to this notion very shortly but go with it for now). In third and fourth year university, my high grades returned. Yes, the anxiety was still there, but it was no longer in control, and it was that reclaiming of power over my own brain that allowed me to continue to progress. At that stage, I had become open to allowing others to help me through sharing and talking about my (and their) experiences. And the benefits of this couldn't be better encapsulated than by just how much more I have grown as a person (both in continuing to overcome anxiety and more generally) in the last year since meeting my amazing boyfriend who, from the very start, has just **got** it. But as he would say, I got myself to that place of allowing him to help me. You never have to do it alone, but you do need to prioritise yourself enough to get to that place where you're receptive to changing your mind.*

Anxiety is horrendous, and it's scary how powerful it can feel - trust me, I've been there and know only too well how non-existent the way out can seem. But it only has as much control as you allow it to. Every day, remind yourself of how powerful your brain is, and that anxiety is only a temporary state that you can absolutely overcome. Just as I did with my body in physically recovering, accept the factors in your life that you cannot control, and focus on what you can. Once you have something to so tangibly remind yourself of your brain power (for me, the gym), overcoming those mental barriers will seem so much more achievable.

The good news is, you're reading this book. In doing so, it is my aim to help you to do all of this. I'm not a psychologist and don't claim to be, but what I am is a very deep-thinking person with a very stubborn mind - if I have come to believe in all of this, then trust me, you should too!

To avoid deterring people from reading this who I think really need to, I didn't want to make the gym a focus. As much as it set off my recovery - as much as I would encourage ANYONE who is suffering to commit to physical exercise towards eradicating forever - the hours I spent rethinking my own mentality (with the help of my boyfriend I should add) played a much bigger part in my recovery than the gym alone. And in any case, it was my brain and mindset that controlled any of the gym progress that encouraged the further mental growth. As such, the book is comprised mainly of general thoughts on anxiety, with some thoughts given to the gym aspect at the end.

Forget the "old" you

2013 - Life was easy and nothing was hard.
2014 - Contracted the viral illness, lost 5 stone and became
      consumed by anxiety from the trauma. Suddenly,
      EVERYTHING was hard.

Literally all I can remember from then is talking about not being the "old me". I would sit in the doctors or multiple therapy rooms that I tried and tell them I just want to be back to the "old me". I obsessed over trying to emulate that person.

But that was never going to get me anywhere, and I only wish that I could go back and tell myself that. The past was safe, and it became my obsession. My ego was desperately trying to return to the security of the familiar. But in that very mindset I was 100% shooting myself in the foot by preventing myself from ever actually looking at my situation to work out how I could help myself *now*. Anyone who tried to help me at that point was talking to a wall because I could never actually process this new person (the one broken by anxiety) that they were talking about. No therapist could help me back then.

Having said that, something one of them said to me said definitely made something click in my head. One day, after one of my "old me" rants, she blankly said, "well I'm not who I was in 2013 ". That's when I realised.

Now, after years of developing this through reading, talking to those close to me, and resolving my own mental dissonance, the flaws in that thinking are even clearer. If you experience some form of mental struggle, it's the result of some sort of trauma (regardless of whether you know what it is). Anxiety is a messenger, a survival response, trying to tell you something is up, so it can't ever exist without trauma. And the thing is, trauma changes you. You can 100% recover from it, but you aren't going to be the same. How could you be? It's like changing the settings on your car and expecting it to drive the exact same. But here's the key - you can decide whether to see that as a negative or as a positive.

And for me, with the help of some amazing people, I have come to see it as the latter. It might seem overly optimistic, but I really believe that if you have the disposition to suffer mentally, you also have the capability to experience life at a deeper level than some. And that's how I feel now; sure, being the "old me" was a breeze, but I can honestly say that the me of today is so much more grateful for every day, and because of it, life is so much more rewarding, fulfilling, and pleasing.

If you find yourself wishing you could go back to the "old" you, it is time to change that thinking.

Take it from me; I've absolutely been "there", but I now KNOW that "here" is the place to be. Because you can make "here" look like whatever you want it to.

After all, every single year, 95% of the atoms in your body are entirely replaced. How could you ever stay the same old you?

What even is "anxiety"?

There's a very simple answer to this - anxiety is the result of an unrealistic desire to try and control things you can't control. Without detracting from the severity of its consequences, that is all it is.

Panic happens when you don't feel in control of your environment.

Overthinking is caused by obsessively considering lots of different possible scenarios, and ultimately, it's the realisation that you can't control them which causes stress.

Obsessive behaviours are an attempt to give regulation to an irregular world.

Self-doubt or negative self-talk occurs because we worry about how other people are seeing us, and to cover all grounds, we assume the worst - again, it's linked to us trying to control the uncontrollable.

But if you can let go of that desire to control, then you allow yourself to begin towards true peace and ease. What you can control is how you see and think of things - to perfect that takes time, but by surrendering and realising how many things you cannot control and thus shouldn't even try to, you will free up a lot of mental energy.

It takes practise, but it is possible. Try to work on it a little a day - in various environments, pause and think. Point out to yourself just how much you cannot control; try to catch yourself as you begin to think about trying to. The more you highlight to yourself how often a lack of control is inevitable, the less you will feel the need to push for it. More importantly though, in the same pause, remind yourself of what you can control - how you are seeing things.

Anxiety is a habit

It's a bad thinking habit. That's it.

And that's not to undermine how horrific it is and how amazing you are if you are fighting it every day, but to disempower it towards giving you back control. Because it's not a simplification - its absolutely true. Every horror that comes with anxiety is caused by a thought that you yourself come up with.

See anxiety as something happening "to" you, and you give it control and things won't get better. But see it as a habit of thinking that (through no fault of your own) you have developed, and you completely flip the cards and allow yourself to begin to heal.

Everything we experience in life is literally the results of our own thoughts. We can't experience anything without a thought process. If only we could control every one of these we have?

But that is just it - we can. It might not feel like it right now, and I know exactly how unlikely it will sound if you are in a place that I've been in before. But believe me when I say that you CAN train your mind. It just takes time, commitment, self-education and patience.

Start small. Listen to the voices in your head with objectivity, always bearing in mind that the thoughts might not be true or coming from the "real" you, but instead are likely to be arising through bad habits.

Regain control of your thoughts, and you move from being able to distract from anxiety, to being able to prevent it altogether. Prevention is always better than reaction.

Anxiety isn't a part of you

This time last year my mental goal had become to find ways to cope with anxiety. The overwhelming narrative in my head had become that anxiety had become such a part of me that the only thing to do was learn ways to distract from it or dull the symptoms. I spoke about "my" anxiety. It was part of me (or so I thought), part of my identity and I had submitted to its wrath. I would say it "just came over me without reason." It was in total control.

Now, I can see how wrong and unhelpful that thinking was, and what proves that to me is the crazy difference in my wellbeing and mindset from a year ago to now. As I can now see it, anxiety is not a thing you catch, and it never has to be a permanent thing. It is a thing, or set of behaviours, that manifest in the face of some sort of trauma. Invest enough time into yourself, whether that is alone or with the help of those close to you, to find out what it is that's not working for you - what it is that is causing dissonance in your head, whether it's your job, a relationship, something placing external pressure on you, or even something missing from your life - and you can absolutely overcome it.

Yes, it's true that it's impossible to ever say you are totally "there" or ever will be - that you will never get another bad day or bad spell of anxiety. But it will never be permanent, and the thing is, if you see it as that - if you identify with it, see it as a part of you that you are going to have to learn to deal with for the rest of your life - then that is what it and you will become. It's a self-fulfilling prophecy.

Don't picture that for yourself. Picture yourself as the ultimate person you want to become, free of suffering and pain, and you'll set yourself up in the best possible environment to become that.

Anxiety is so horrifically overwhelming, that in the depths of it, it's hard to envisage that. Trust me, I've been there. It's hard to see any possible way out.

But please believe me when I can ASSURE you that you can overcome this. Don't submit to it, because you are SO much more than it.

Reframe anxiety

One of the biggest things you can do is to stop saying that you "have" anxiety. By doing this you are giving it power, and subconsciously, some part of you is giving in to it and deep down will be less inclined to fight it. Instead, simply recognise that, in response to some sort of trauma in the past (again, you may or may not know what this is), you are experiencing some anxious tendencies. These can be horrific, all consuming, and life changing, but they are NOT permanent, and again, the key is to not see them as negatives.

Anxiety arises when your body wants to tell you something is off. This is a good thing - it wants you to better yourself. Try and see it as a fire alarm in your house. You wouldn't just sit and give in to the sound of the alarm: you would switch it off. But even better than this would be to find the source of the fire. So yes, do what you can to make yourself feel better day to day (for me, exercise is biggest thing), but remember that if you don't put out the fire, the alarm will come back. But if, when you are in a calmer headspace, you can begin to look into yourself and identify your triggers, you can progressively remove the alarm altogether. You really can.

I'm not saying it's easy. The truth is that you might have to go through some more bad to get to the even better. But you owe that to yourself.

As unorthodox as this might sound, the next time you begin to feel anxious, try to convince yourself that it's actually excitement you are feeling. Excitement for that better and more fulfilled version of you. This will put you so much more in control than simply surrendering to what you think of as your condition.

Dealing with anxiety sucks, it really does, but try to reframe it as above, and remember that every day you fight through it, you are carving a better you to come - one who can appreciate and enjoy everything and every day so much more. Your once-horrific anxiety WILL one day be a blessing.

You will always be stronger than it

It's frightening just how strong anxiety can feel. It can feel like it has taken your life. It's so easy to let yourself believe that, with no legible way to ever vanquish its grip, this will be you forever.

It's not so easy to remember, though, that these anxious behaviours came from somewhere inside of YOU. Nobody is born with them, nobody gives them to you, and actually, as you now know, they have good intentions in the way that they arise as messengers to try and tell you something is wrong. Whether you know what it is or not, some event(s) from your past have caused today's suffering. Acknowledge that these super strong and influential feelings and responses were actually made by YOU, and the task of reversing them seems more doable.

Because the thing is, if you are prone to anxiety, it actually says a lot about the diligence and intricacy of your brain. Anxiety arises when you feel out of control of external forces - but really, nobody in the world has control of these things, so why do only some suffer? To me, it's because they feel things at a deeper level, and so are more aware of just how much of life they don't have control over. Whether that's a positive or not is up to you (think about accepting the unchangeable), but what it does mean, is that you patently have the ability to operate at a deep level of subconscious thought. You went deep enough in there to teach your brain to react in certain ways to certain situations, so regardless of if it feels like it now or not, you absolutely have the assiduity to form better habits. Give yourself practise at positive affirmations and challenging instinctive behaviours, and with time, you can regain control. This last fact has often brought me comfort: your suffering is due only to a depth of emotion that you feel that is beyond that of many others. Cling on to that and let the knowledge that the bad days are only preparing you for MUCH better days to come help you through.

You really are SO much stronger than you think. Believe in that, and you can unquestionably redefine your mind.

Dissociation

Do you know what dissociation is? You may have heard of forms of dissociative disorder, and whilst they are related, I think it's important to know that you can still experience the phenomenon without having a disorder. Commonly, this will be caused by anxiety (as with me). In this case, spells will usually be shorter lived, but this makes them no less unpleasant/worthy of attention!

Symptoms:

- *Feeling disconnected from yourself and not really "there" throughout your day. You may feel as though it's like you are just floating through the day without really feeling or experiencing much*
- *Feeling suddenly distant from those around you*
- *Experiencing periods in which you lose concept of time - one minute you are watching Netflix, the next, 4 hours have gone by and when you look back, it doesn't feel like you've actually lived those 4 hours*
- *Having unusually scatty or forgetful times. You are asked to buy milk when at the shops but totally forget, or you may do something that would normally be totally irresponsible and unlike you, such as leaving the hob on after cooking and burning a tea towel or bumping your car straight into a bollard. You might get total mind blanks when you are thinking about anything from what someone said to you or*

what someone's name is

- *Losing sense of judgement in terms of what is safe or morally acceptable. You may drive around on very little fuel thinking "it will be fine" when you wouldn't normally*
- *Feeling emotionally numb, or less caring than you normally are*

If these sound familiar, you might be dissociating (you also might not be but it's worth considering). It doesn't make you broken - it's a natural reaction. Basically, dissociation is a coping mechanism. In times of stress/bad anxiety, it makes sense for your body to shut down some awareness, so this is exactly what it does, and thus comes a disconnection between your memory, consciousness, identity, and thoughts. While normally your brain processes events together, during dissociation, it doesn't, leaving you with a feeling of disconnection from the present.

If you experience this, as always, it's important to look for the cause of the stress. Anxiety really is a messenger. Similarly, though, it's important to be able to relieve the symptoms. So, what will help?

☆ Tell someone close to you that you think you might be experiencing this. This is important because due to the nature of it i.e., a disconnection between your experiences and how they are processed, sometimes it's hard to recognise it in yourself

☆ Practise grounding strategies to bring yourself back to the present

☆ Mindfulness practices

☆ Journal - write about your experiences and how they made you feel. This should help you recognise if you haven't been fully aware

Again, this is in no way constituent of professional help. But I hope that in sharing things like this I can make you feel less alone.

Rationalising anxiety

The ultimate goal towards not giving anxiety any control is being able to ignore it. But that **doesn't** happen straight away. It takes a lot of practise. At the start you are still going to get unwanted and intrusive thoughts. You will overthink, overgeneralise, catastrophise, and essentially, it's these that lead to the panic attacks, obsessive behaviours, and the "lump in your throat" feeling.

To me, the most important thing you can do is be able to call out anxiety for what it is. Name it, realising it's separate from your rational thought. Realise you don't "have" anxiety, but you just experience anxious tendencies (for good reason). Because as you've already read, that's all anxiety is... a behavioural response.

The problem is, once anxiety has infiltrated your life, because you are controlled by what happens externally, you don't trust yourself. With so much self-doubt, and with so much being decided by your subconscious (which is where anxiety grows) it can be near impossible to trust yourself if you tell yourself that your thought aren't rational - that they are anxious thoughts - never mind be able to distinguish them as that in the first place. If you feel like your life has been taken over by anxiety, it's **so** important to resolve this issue. Once you realise that when you begin to worry, the likelihood is that your thoughts aren't rational, it's a lot easier to calm yourself down. Try these two things towards doing so next time you feel overcome:

1. Write down all of your concerns. Later, ideally with the help of a loved one, return to the list and mark any that were not necessary worries. I remember doing this one day, and of a list of 12 worries, only one was a real problem. Once I had calmed myself down, it was so much easier to deal with this one issue rather than ruminate about the other 11.

2. Talk to someone you trust and voice all of your concerns. As well as feeling better for sharing them, this will probably also lead to you realising that what your anxious mind saw as a catastrophe likely wasn't that at all.

Whichever way you do it, with enough acknowledgement of the likelihood that your worries are simply anxiety talking, you (and your subconscious) will become more aware of the nature of intrusive thoughts. With practise, it will become first easier, then automatic, to call out anxiety when it begins to take control. At this point, you'll start to regain control of your life by bringing yourself back to your consciousness, or rather, being able to trust it again. Once you can decide the rationality of a concern, it is much easier to either disregard it, or deal with it in a headspace free of anxious inclinations.

In essence, you need to fight the disease of the unconscious with conscious awareness, and this will become so much easier if you let someone you trust in.

The danger of "disorder"

How would you define a "disordered" mentality? At what exact point would you say that your mental state has gone from "normal" to "disordered"?

In reality, judging how healthy your mind is usually requires a comparison to others - a comparison to "normal". Whilst it's amazing that mental health is becoming so much more recognised, with this also comes a danger - that suddenly, any mental differences are labelled as a "disorder". And the thing is, if you do notice that you aren't like others, a big part of the reason that you suffer for it may be these labels. Again, it's a self-fulfilling prophecy. If you are told that certain feelings are indicative of a disorder, you are going to think of, and live out, those times as negative.

But who is to say that your differing mentality is "disordered"? Something to always remember is that it's easier for the pharmacy world (your GP) to jump to prescribing medication to ease symptoms. It's easier for authorities to diagnose "disorder" than to change a whole culture to better suit individual needs.

It's easier for the government to manage a society of people who are medicated towards being as "normal" as possible. (That's in no way to dismiss the need for medication - it's fact that it's what some people need and always will.)

But what if, instead of desperately trying to chase "normal", you embraced your differences, and creatively channelled them in to becoming amazingly unique?

There is of course the blunt and indisputable fact that if you are suffering you need to change your thinking habits, but the question is, who are you going to let direct what that change is? Society? A GP? Or are you going to look into yourself and your life to work out what it is that actually isn't working for you?

What if you just don't like nightclubs or crowded places?

What if you need constant activity in your day over sitting in an office?

Just because you can't seem to get by like "normal" people in a 9-5 job, just because crowded places often trigger panic, just because your family don't "get" you ... it doesn't necessarily mean you are "disordered".

Mentally illnesses are REAL. But maybe it's time to rethink how we think about them.

You aren't your "disorder".

Bad days

I'm conscious when sharing my experiences that I give the impression that I am totally there - that I never struggle anymore - and that this might make some feel they have a long way to go. This isn't true at all, so here is a reality check: I still get bad days!

"Good vibes only", or "choose happy" have become popular terms. We have evolved into a culture of "positivity", where anything other than being happy is seen as bad. And I think this is to a fault.

Obviously being happy is preferable, but sadness, just as much as joy, is a vital emotion. Otherwise, why would it be a thing? As humans, towards balance and true contentment (not happiness, they're different), we need the contrast of "good" and "bad" (to be returned to later). But in our culture, as soon as we do feel low, we tend to overthink and make unhelpful assumptions. "Bad days" have become the enemy, and the thought of eradicating them seems to be the goal.

But we need sadness. It's in sadness that sometimes we come to realisations about ways we can grow. Ways to make the good days even better. This isn't to say this is something you need to consciously make happen, but even in riding out the bad days, usually something will be going on at a deeper level.

So next time you have a bad day, remember this. Do not think of the day as necessarily "bad", don't overgeneralise and convince yourself that after several days or weeks of feeling good that you must be going backwards, but simply ride through the day in the knowledge that your body knows what it is doing and that the bad days are necessary for better days to come. Think of the bad days as place holders for all the amazing days you will have in your life.

This isn't to say you shouldn't do something to make the bad days better. Of course, doing something to cheer yourself up is good, but what you shouldn't do is let the idea of a bad day set you back at all, or dominate your head space. They're not fun, but bad days are just as ok and (maybe more internally) productive as good days.

So, whatever you're doing on this day, whether it's a good or bad day, trust in your body and remember that everything does happen for a reason.

Fear of judgement should never silence you

I once carried out a poll online which confirmed that there's around an 80% chance that fear of judgement of others would stop people from talking about mental issues (361 voters). Here's why this shouldn't be a thing.

(Want to say first that a) eventually you want to be able to regulate your own emotions, and b) you should be careful of who you accept advice from. But regardless, it's always helpful to open up and get things off your chest, and the reality is that this is the first step in getting yourself professional help if it comes to it.)

SO, if you feel like you need to talk to someone about anxiety etc., it clearly means you are suffering anxiety. The ironic thing though, is that anxiety is the thing that's going to stop you from doing so, as it means you are going to misjudge what others will think, and that's down to three tendencies of anxious people:

1. **Negativity Bias**

    All this means is that you are more likely to focus on negatives in your life rather than positives, and (under another phenomenon called the false consensus bias), you are then likely to look for these things more. For example, if you hinted that you are struggling to someone, and they hesitated a little before responding, this is the biggest and most important thing you would pick up on. You would take this one little reaction, assume it's a negative, overgeneralise it, and within seconds, convince yourself that they are judging you. The reality may be though, that the other person was just taking a few seconds to take in your words and think of the best way to support you.

2. Assuming the worst and catastrophising

This is in a way linked to the first but can be more general. If you are suffering anxiety your body is in fight or flight mode and is going to try and be prepared for the worst at all times. As a result, you are always going to assume the worst-case scenario, and naturally, it will be hard to imagine that by speaking out, you could be put on to the right help and totally turn your life around. Note: anxiety likes the status quo. It wants to conserve your energy and so will always try to deter you from instigating change. But your anxiety (and the ego working alongside it to protect you) doesn't actually know what is good and bad for you. You do. Overrule it and remind yourself that you are so much more than the set of temporary behaviours that are anxiety.

3. Assuming your own perspective on to others

Again, this is linked to the false consensus bias above. Naturally, even non sufferers will, at some deep level, tend towards the assumption that everyone else sees the world just as they do. But if you suffer anxiety, this is going to be even more profound. Again, anxiety wants to prepare you for the absolute worst, so by extension, will cover all grounds by forcing you to think that everyone has the same anxious perspective as you. For example, an anxious tendency is to be hyper aware of how others communicate with you, either in words or body language. Your anxiety then, will tell you that others must be like that too. But remember, even without anxiety, literally no two people ever have the same perspective, and they never will be able to because everyone is totally unique. How other people react to you or anything else is going to be totally dependent on their own personal experiences and value base, so remind yourself that even though your body may try hard to convince you so, just because you analyse everything too deeply, it doesn't mean that other people will too. Approach people with an open mind, whether you are doing so for help or not, reminding yourself that you literally have no idea what is going on in their head.

Basically, the take-away from these is that you should never be scared to open up to someone you trust. Your anxiety will try and tell you and convince you that it's a bad idea, but as a human being, you have the higher level of intelligence to override this, push past your conditioning, and make decisions that's are good for you. And the thing is, if you do open up, and receive a bad reaction (i.e., judgement) from that other person, then one of two things is true:

a)   *They themselves, are not totally mentally secure, and so they wouldn't be helpful to speak to anyway (harsh but true - these people need time and space). (This would be different if that person is open about their issues meaning you can relate and comfort each other, but if they're not open or in denial, they aren't the people to be talking to).*

b)   *They simply aren't worth your time. There are so many people in the world who want to help, so don't waste time on anyone else. And the thing is, after a few baby steps, as you become more open to help, you will begin to attract likeminded people. Trust me, I didn't always have such an amazing network of support!*

If you're struggling today, even just a little, please don't do it alone.

Breaking anxious habits

As I have already said, anxiety, at its root, is a habit. Lots of habits of faulty patterns of thinking that have arisen due to some sort of trauma. As I have also already said, you may or may not know what this trauma was, but regardless, the principle is the same. Although these patterns are faulty though, it's vital that, under this notion, you never punish yourself for it, but rather, thank yourself. The habits may not help you today, but at one time, at a very basic and existential level, your body developed them to try and protect you. Yes they are faulty, but they are also valid and justified, and your body deserves love for that. Before I go further, here are some examples of such anxious habits:

- Nail biting
- Binge eating or drinking
- Smoking
- Pulling hair
- Picking skin (excoriation)
- Compulsive shopping
- Negative self-talk
- Negative self-image
- Assuming the worst
- Taking blame for what isn't your fault
- Taking on too much responsibility for others
- Paranoia
- Self-sacrifice
- Catastrophising situations
- Overthinking
- Comparison to others

- Negativity bias
- Dwelling on the past
- Obsessive behaviours

The problem, our bodies do not like change, and that is why such behaviours - formed during times of stress or the subsequent period of trying to rebalance - stick and become habits. Your body, at a biological level, will always aim to preserve energy. Sticking to the learned "normal" requires much less energy than challenging beliefs, so this is what it naturally chooses.

And unfortunately, if you are suffering anxiety, this is compounded; anxiety arises and thrives on a looming sense of threat, and so every day, your guard is going to be even more heightened, and even more of your energy is going to be put it to self-protection and preservation, and anything that contests your current state.

And that's why habits (especially anxious habits) are so hard to kick. But the key thing to realise, is that just as you learned the negative behaviours, so too can you unlearn them, or learn better ones. Some of the examples in the above list are typical habits, but some you may not immediately think of as a habit. But that is the answer here - rather than concluding that your negative self-talk is merely due to, and under the control of, anxiety, and so by extension giving in to external factors, realise that, just like nail biting, they are behavioural habits that you can always unlearn. It just takes some commitment and improvement in small steps.

So, how do you do this? What you **don't** want to do is tell yourself you are going to stop all of it right now: "I will never again assume everything is my fault"; "I will never again compare myself to my non-suffering sister". That will not work. At first, do not even commit to any change, but rather, step back, observe and notice.

The first step lies in being able to acknowledge the bad habit; recognise it for what it is and tell yourself that it is just this. At the beginning it might be helpful to remind yourself that it comes from anxiety, but ideally, you want to move away from this, and instead, remind yourself again and again that it's a behaviour that you ultimately are 100% in control of. With time, if you do this enough, you can teach your body that these unhelpful behaviours aren't conducive to your wellbeing. It's at **this** stage that you can then begin to commit to change... *slowly.*

It's not helpful to go cold turkey because that isn't realistic and will only lead to more self-frustration and resentment, but over time, commit to consciously work at reducing the instances of the habits, and most importantly, **reward** and **praise** yourself when you manage to do so. Don't play this down - as much as I believe that everyone has the power to control their behaviours, this doesn't mean that it doesn't take a tonne of strength and willpower to do so. Imagine the way you would praise a small child for using a potty for the first time and apply this to yourself.

In opposition to the self-view and degradation that anxiety will push for, grant yourself the understanding and compassion that you would give others.

"Who told you that?

You've already read about rationalising anxiety, and in this explained that it's useful to entrust in someone at first to help. But eventually, you want to be able to do it yourself. You should ultimately be able to control your reactions to the world without relying on ANYTHING external.

A really simple way of doing this, once you're good at calling out when you have an anxious thought, is to ask yourself if you can actually prove the idea. Basically, whenever you notice yourself begin to feel anxious - whether it's anxious that someone is annoyed at you, that people are talking about you, that people think you are unworthy, that people think you are ugly - ask yourself, "who told you that?". The reality is that the majority of the time, nobody did. Or rather, only the anxiety did.

But anxiety is so all consuming, so human like (it originates in a human mind so it will be) that it's scarily good at convincing you otherwise and does so without you realising it. The key: separate your true self in your head from the wrath of anxiety. Give it a separate entity that is both temporary and removable. This way, you can still trust in yourself (crucial for self-regulation) without trusting every thought you have. Because until you are healed, a lot of your thoughts will be the anxiety talking and it's vital that you realise their fallacies.

You do need to get to the stage of recognising an anxious thought, of 100% knowing your own mind to be able to do this, but once you can, and once you can make it a daily habit, then you can absolutely teach your brain that your anxious thoughts do not parallel reality.

Master this and you are another step further to being in control of the way your body reacts to everything in the world, and anxiety, panic and unnecessary, self-inflicted stress become a thing of past you. And trust me, it feels amazing. With so much less energy being spent on battling with intrusive, false thoughts, you free up so much to be able to commit to finding happiness in every day.

The "Caveman Effect"

In this day and age everything has become so advanced and complex, whether in terms of technology, knowledge, cultures or relationships. It's really no wonder that, as humans, originating in caveman times where the only priorities in a day were literally to eat and sleep, many of us have ended up with our heads in a bit of a mess. Yes, we have evolved, but to me it's always worth remembering that originally, we were built to deal with so much less, and so expecting yourself to deal with the challenges of today without any conscious work on your own mind is never going to work.

Often, our minds still show signs of a caveman mentality (that black and white thinking where the only priority was getting food and surviving). This is clearly not applicable today. Put a caveman in the 21st century during a global pandemic and literally everything would be a threat - the fight or flight response would kick in and he would be anxious and disturbed beyond functioning. It might seem far-fetched, but try to remember that in many ways, our brains are remarkably similar to how theirs were back then.

The "caveman effect" shows us just how unevolved the human mind still is and how easily it can malfunction unless being constantly upgraded. These upgrades require you to consciously be aware that your brain is no longer functioning to serve your current situation and take steps to recognise that you have the capacity to restructure the way your own mind works.

Don't expect yourself just to be able to deal with everything naturally or get annoyed/hate on yourself if you start to struggle and can't work out why. Some people might never have to deal with this idea, but the reality is that most of us, with our biological roots lying in caveman times, will need to teach our brains a few things in order to best survive life as it is today.

No matter how intelligent, confident, sociable, or privileged you are, we are all human, and at some level, we are all still cavepeople. What we have that they did not though, is the intelligence, information, tools and support to be able to train our brains to best serve our lives.

The Self-Analysis Trap

Self-reflection is really healthy. As you've read, it's important to look back and understand the roots of your behaviour. Remember, the way you react to things is always because of your past experiences and the conditioning which arose as a result. Towards both self-acceptance and improvement, analysis of this is needed. We are also taught to be self-reflective as kids, as our parents taught us to take responsibility for our actions.

But, if, like me, you're a deep thinker, this can become complicated - there's a point where it can become too much. You can fall into the self-analysis trap in which you expect yourself to be able to both understand and control everything that happens to you. But you can't ever do this. Because to truly understand every one of your own motives, you would need to truly understand everything others do to you, and this will simply never be doable. So when you inevitably fail yourself of this expectation, self-degradation, annoyance and a negative self-image become all too possible.

Sometimes, things will happen in the external world for reasons that you will never understand, and so sometimes, rather than analysing every feeling that arises in reaction to it, the best thing you can do is to **accept what is**. In such situations, it would be helpful to, rather than focus on that external event that upset you, focus on learning mechanisms that keep you calm and can help you return to a positive, calm state (e.g., positive affirmations, or switching off your overactive, super analytical brain and simply listening to music or smashing a weights session).

Because the thing is, nobody EVER analyses other people as much as they analyse themselves, so do you really always need to go so far?

This is not to take away from the importance of introversion towards understanding yourself. This is SO helpful, and one of the biggest things that has helped me. What I am saying though, is that *there is a line between healthy and driving yourself mad*. Too much of anything really is bad! If you are like the past me, who prided myself in self-control and never showing struggle, letting go of constant self-analysis and rationalization can be scary. BUT, by accepting that you cannot know or explain your whole self, you liberate yourself from the constant burden of rumination. You are free to control what you can control - your reactions to thoughts - and to let the rest come and go.

Some reassurance

Anxiety is intense, and without a question causes a negativity bias - an intense focus and emphasis placed on negative thoughts and events. This makes it so easy to think that there is *nothing* positive to consider; that there is no hope. But there just is. I really have been at rock bottom and want anyone who reads this to believe that things can always, always get better! Let's reel it back a little today and re-cap. Here are three things to remember today that have helped me most the last year:

1. You are **not** alone and never will be. 1 in 4 people will struggle mentally at some point in their lives. Think about that the next time you are in Tesco or the likes - a quarter of the people in the building will at some point be able to relate to what you're going through. Anxiety or similar can be so overwhelming due to the survival mode your body goes in to, making it so easy to lose perspective and become trapped in your own head, as if you are the only person in the world to have gone through this. No matter how bad it gets, you are never the only one.

2. You can absolutely retrain your mind. I never used to believe this - I thought I was too deep in anxiety and that my mind was too stubborn to be changed. I didn't believe in all the mind training I read about. But I was wrong. Every unhelpful or anxious behaviour you have now is merely that - a behaviour that you have learned - and just as your mind learned it, you can unlearn it with practise and time.

3. Once you can get to a place of accepting what is and surrendering to trying to control what you can't, life becomes **so** much easier.

Realistic Positivity

Too much emphasis on positivity can be toxic, and the simple reason for this is that it to be positive 24/7 would require us to be able to control our surroundings. But with another 7.5 billion people in the world - or even the 2 or 3 people you live with - that's never going to be possible.

That doesn't mean positivity doesn't have a huge part to play in happiness though - it's just about how you use it. Realistically, or toxically.

REALISTIC POSITIVITY is:

❤ Having high hopes/long term expectations of yourself
❤ Affirmations and focusing on what you are grateful for
❤ Focusing on the relative good in a bad situation
❤ Praising yourself when you achieve a goal
❤ Speaking to yourself nicely
❤ Making choices to do things you enjoy

TOXIC POSITIVITY is:

❤ Expecting to be happy 24/7 - it's not going to happen and when you have a bad day you will likely beat yourself up for it or see it as a setback when really, it's a natural part of life. Bad moods will be blown out of proportion and ironically you will suffer more through them.

💜 Chasing a goal because it seemed like the right thing to do or it makes other people happy, when actually it's just not for you. Accepting when something isn't working will 100% lead to more future success than trying to push through by "staying positive" and actually shooting yourself in the foot.

💜 Reading too much into a bad day because it's not what you planned. Sadness is natural and it is ok - your body knows what it is doing and deep down, healing and growing will be happening in these times. Distract yourself on bad days, but you don't always have to fight it.

💜 Striving to appear happy just because other people do - comparing to any single person never does and never will make sense.

💜 Denying your own reality in an attempt to "stay positive", which will likely lead to dissociation, loss of identity, internal dissonance. You can't progress your life without being grounded in, and ACCEPTING, your own reality.

The bottom line - approach life with positivity, but when things don't go to plan, the most important thing (instead of forced positivity) is acceptance of what is and the resulting formation of realistic plans to turn bad to good.

An over-fixation on "positive thinking" is detrimental

At the most basic level, humans are built, and function for, survival. It's natural then that the world is constantly scanned and examined for threat, whether that is physical danger, potential health issues, social embarrassment, financial risk, or anything else.

And that's why a constant stream of so called "negative thoughts" are inevitable. This is an idea I encountered in reading Russ Harris' 2008 work.[1] Think of it like a radio station, constantly broadcasting all possible threats in your life. It's always going to be playing away in the background, and that's normal.

What the "positive thinking" movement encourages, is the creation of a second radio station - the "positive station". Play it louder than the above "negative station" to drown it out and eventually you will forget about it - right?

The problem is, for me anyway, if I were to play two radio stations at an initial same volume, I would find it very hard to focus on either of them, never mind be able to pick out the desirable "positive" broadcast.

---

[1] Harris, R. (2008). *The Happiness Trap: Stop Struggling, Start Living.* Robinson Publishing.

Your "negative" station will never switch off. It's there to protect you. Instead of trying to drown it out, the key for me lies in acceptance, and being able to separate your calm and rational self from your "thinking" self (i.e., the constant radio broadcaster).

More than that however, a thought shouldn't really be seen as "positive" or "negative" (we will come back to this idea) - instead, practise questioning how helpful the thought is to your life. If it is, acknowledge it: if it's not, step back and let it go.

Ideally, every time you have a thought, you want to be able to simply observe it for just that - a thought. It's not always right, and it's not always rational. This won't come overnight - but it will come with practise. Whenever you have a thought, step back and view it as an outsider. Then, before any emotional reaction, decide whether or not it is helpful to your life.

Nihilism and how it can help you

Nihilism is the realisation that, in reality, we all die one day. It's the acknowledgment of how tiny a part we play in the big(gest) sense of the world.

How does this make you feel? Commonly, it reaps negative emotions - feelings of pointlessness or a lack of motivation to do anything. What's the point when everyone dies the same? If you get caught in this thinking it can be hard to find worth in each day. This is called pessimistic nihilism and is a pattern of thinking that commonly leads to poor mental health. Always striving to achieve some unknown and pointless end goal can mess with your head.

Fortunately, though, you can choose the alternative - optimistic nihilism - and for me, this is a perspective really worth considering. Still being nihilism, it's still based on the idea that really, life doesn't have much purpose. With enough practise and intention however, this can be the best realisation you can make. With the right thinking, what used to be feelings of pointlessness and low worth can become feelings of freedom and calm. What a lack of meaning in the universe actually means is that you are free to create your own meaning. It means you have time, in fact a whole **life**time to find what makes *you* happy. Not what society says should make you happy, and not what the rules of the world say should do so.

Because there are no rules, and life doesn't come with any instructions or timelines. For me though, this has come to bring a massive sense of calm, and, ironically, purpose. Your purpose is literally to find happiness.

What it also means is you have time: time to work on yourself, to slow down your pace and enjoy the little things, and to spend meaningful time with loved ones. You have time to try things, even if they don't work out.

Nihilism can do one of two things: strip your life of purpose or fill your life with purpose (to find what actually makes you happy). We seem to grow up thinking there are rules and timelines to life. But to me it's pretty ignorant for humans, who are so tiny in the context of the world, to think they can assign these rules.

We really have no clue what our purpose is here. **But let that liberate and console you over anything else.**

Rethink mental "illness"

This one is short but requires some deep thought. Read it a few times, let it sink in, and discuss it with as many people as possible.

Back in the 18th century when societies were in their primitive years, those presenting mental differences - who today have become the "mentally ill" - were actually seen as beneficial to society. Their creative minds and "interesting pallor and sense of passion" rendered them valuable contributors to the development and revolution of the world.

Idiosyncrasies of personalities weren't immediately seen as pathological.

And the thing is, in my opinion, now more than ever, our world - its politics, its economics, its social cohesion - is in need of large-scale revolution and change.

Maybe it's time we shake up our presumptions and what we think we know about anyone not exactly like others.

Mental Health through Philosophy

As you know, anxious thoughts are not rational thoughts. Our brain does not always get it right - so much of our biological make up is still rooted in the survival instincts that were necessary in ancient times. As such, it learns habits fuelled by our ego who is always out to protect us and isn't always able to distinguish which of these are actually now counterintuitive or problematic to life in the 21st century. But like any other sustained thought pattern, these habits become enmeshed into our subconscious to the point of being automatic thoughts.

Luckily though, our brain has evolved to be so much more than instinctive - what is needed, and what you can learn to do, is critical thought, and that's where Philosophy comes in. Essentially, philosophy is the practise of questioning everything you see and hear - it challenges assumptions and brings truth in to question - and that's exactly what you need to do to begin to regain control over anxious habits. Get into the HABIT of asking yourself:

How do I know that? Where is that thought coming from? Can I prove that's true?

...whenever an anxious thought begins to creep in. I promise you, once done enough to the point of being an automatic response to anxiety, it's life changing. So much of life today is automatic and information is there in an instant when we need it. Philosophical thinking then, is diminishing, and it's so easy to go through a day in "instant" mode, without having really critically think about anything at all. But whilst that's a positive in some ways, it clearly isn't for many aspects of mental health (anxiety).

Regain control of that aspect of your brain, and I promise you, anxiety can be on the way out.

Do you identify with anxiety?

When it comes to something as abstract and only conceptual as anxiety, it can often seem much easier to simply identify with it and label yourself rather than face it head on and get to the root of the issue: "I'm just an anxious person so I should just accept it and learn to live with it."

I totally get that, and of course it's good to name it and talk to others with similar experiences. But what you cannot do, is let the anxiety become a part of your identity, because that way, your ego (and hence the anxiety caused by its protective intentions) will come to control you and it becomes harder and harder to break free from it. Perhaps counter-intuitively, that's what it wants.

Put simply, our egos are obsessed with creating a strong identity to cling to in order to feel a sense of belonging. It might identify as belonging to the group of "readers", "film buffs", "gym go-ers", or "gin drinkers". This isn't always a bad thing: but sometimes it is. Too often, a convenient thing to cling to and identify with becomes illness - usually, mental illness.

And once it does this. it won't want to let go. Remember, our egos don't have a consciousness to decipher between what is good for us and our lived experiences and what isn't - it purely runs on survival instincts. What it doesn't realise then, is that with every day that it identifies with "anxiety", the person it lives in will suffer more and more.

Anxiety isn't a part of you; you don't belong to the group of "anxiety sufferers". That's the easy way out, and what your ego wants you to think to protect you, but I promise you, it will get you nowhere.

Acknowledge that you have developed anxious tendencies, but never label yourself or submit to the "illness".

Teach your subconscious through sharing your experiences

One thing that helped me massively was starting an Instagram page in which I began to share my experiences and talk through my evolving thought processes. Through trying to help others grow, I ended up doing a whole lot of growing myself. I spent a lot of time thinking about the reasons for this.

Essentially, I think that in really thinking about my own thoughts and having to put them in to some sort of order that other people could relate to, I have been subconsciously teaching myself too. It's like that in talking to my audience, I have been talking to my subconscious (where all anxiety and unhealthy habits originate) too, and every day, have been progressively making the ideas more and more concrete within myself. Kind of a literal form of forming a habit. It's well known that to really understand something, you have to be able to communicate it to another, and that's my advice for today:

If you have someone close who you trust, make a habit of talking though your feelings daily, or rather, the reasoning behind them. Tell them what about anything you did which made you feel better. Tell them what made things worse. For me, the more that you talk about these things, the more your body will internalise them at that critical subconscious level where thoughts originate, and the easier you will form new good habits. Because the thing is, your subconscious is of course amazing, but it doesn't distinguish between helpful or unhelpful feelings - it literally just runs on that need for survival. But our world is so much more than that, and that is why you need to teach it to accommodate for that. (If you're not comfortable talking to someone in such real terms yet, try journaling. This way, you are still making yourself organise your thoughts into something discernible. If you do this though, make sure you are reading it back and taking it all in from an outside perspective. Imagine you're talking to that subconscious.)

Your thoughts really do determine every bit of your reality - master them, and you're on your way.

You can't change your past

You really do not know your own strength until you need to.

People say that your past doesn't define you. But it kind of does - just not exhaustively and exclusively. Everything that happens in your past of course affects you today, and to deny that isn't logical or helpful. What is helpful is to decide HOW you let it define you.

If I hadn't come across struggle in the past, I may have never joined the gym. I definitely wouldn't have the understanding of myself, others and the world that I do today and may have never known my own strength either physically or mentally.

What happened in your past happened - no, you can't change it and yes, it does in a way define who you are today. What you can do though is decide how it does so. You can let it affect you progressively over time in either a negative or positive way. Both take the same energy; it just depends on which you choose.

It might be horrible to realise that after any sort of trauma or hardship you will not be the same person anymore. But stick in, and I promise you that one day you will actually be grateful for what it made you become. With new depths of understanding the world really can be a special place.

Negative thoughts are inevitable

"Negative thoughts will never lead to a happy life". This is true, but what also won't make a happy life is unrealistic expectations.

Negative thoughts are inevitable. As humans who aren't born in a state anything like they will die, progressively growing and evolving is central to our nature, and as a result, we will always naturally have an idea in our head of a future self we want to become. Negative thoughts, from this perspective, are merely the result of the dissonance between the two.

Of course, we can spin negative thoughts into positive affirmations of who we want to become, but that should never go so far as that any negative thoughts are seen as failings of yourself as a "mindful" person. The reality is that there is always going to be discord between the person you are now and the one you want to become, and so really, negative thoughts WILL happen, and to totally deny them only creates further inner conflict.

So, what, we should just accept negative thoughts? No. For me, the key is to change your mindset - to see yourself as two distinct parts in order to not identify with every single negative thought you have. Imagine:

a) the reactive, emotional human in you that is always growing and evolving, and

b) the ultimate self you want to become.

That is, whenever you catch yourself thinking negatively of yourself (for example "I'm such an idiot forgetting to pay that bill"), literally remove yourself from that person, envisage yourself as that future ultimate self, and observe the negative thought from the outside for exactly what it is: the human in you that is still growing and improving.

What this also means is that negative thoughts are NOT always true or necessary - they are coming from a self that is still learning and founded partly on emotion so how could they be? Don't identify with that chastising self but recognise that you are capable of being that much better, ultimate higher self. Become that person, and let the negative thought do what it will.

You can never fully control your thoughts

As I have said before, you will never be able to control the external world - all you can do it manage how you react to it. But what isn't as popularly thought, is that you can't actually, as much as you may want to, control your internal world either.

Again, as I have said before, negative thoughts happen, and fighting them or chastising yourself when they continue to do so will only cause further inner conflict. But here's an experiment I adapted from Dr Russ Harris' idea[2] to prove it:

As you read this, I challenge you not to think about your favourite snack. Don't picture it sitting on a plate in front of you, don't think about how good it tastes, and don't hear how it sounds when you eat it.

Could you do it? The reality is, as much as we might like to think so, we will never have full control of our internal world and thoughts. But, like what happens in the world around us, what we can control is how we react to them and what actions we can take towards modulating how they affect us.

Acceptance of, and allowing safe space for, negative thoughts is the first step towards doing this. Don't fight them and don't let society convince you that you are disordered for having them. Don't fall into the trap.

You are human.

Fighting off unhelpful thoughts

This idea may seem a little cheesy and unrefined but go with it. This is a strategy I have used a lot myself, and it really is a strong tool in overcoming anxiety.

You can have all the good intent in the world, but when those intrusive and anxious thoughts arrive, you're stumped. These can go from small things like "those people are judging me", to bigger things like "I will never feel content again". The thing is, your body thinks these thoughts are helpful, as, in response to past experiences, it thinks you need protecting and so does everything it can to stop you changing the current state of your body. The good news, of course, is that you can teach it otherwise.

What helped me in doing this is quite literally picturing myself fighting off these thoughts in my head or destroying them in some way. It sounds silly, but by envisaging the negative thought as something literally intruding your head (so not actually part of you), and you physically destroying it, you are teaching your brain that a) the thought isn't wanted or helpful, and b) that you are stronger than it.

Picture the negative thought as a punch bag. Then picture you, strong and in control, literally kicking the life out of it. Picture yourself watching the thought explode and burn. Picture whatever works for you, as long as you are the one in control.

---

[2] Harris, R. (2008). *The Happiness Trap: Stop Struggling, Start Living.* Robinson Publishing.

It might sound too literal and silly - I never used to believe in this sort of thing - but please trust me when I say you can train your mind to do anything. It won't happen right away, but if you get into the habit of, whenever you have an intrusive thought, stopping whatever you are doing and focusing all your energy in to picturing yourself destroying and shutting it down (having that image will help ensure that your thoughts don't wander), your brain will learn.

Soon, just as you formed the habit of unhelpful thinking, you will learn the habit of unlearning unhelpful thinking by recognising and getting rid of it.

"Disorder" as a noun

This has been addressed previously, but for me, it's huge and worth revisiting.

Used as a noun, I do not like the term "disorder".

"She has a disorder" - it's in control, it happens TO her, it is permanent, she is faulty and not working properly, and it's probably just a part of her.

To me, for mental health sufferers, the word should only be used as an adjective: "She is experiencing disordered thinking". It's temporary, she is in actually in control of it, it has arisen through some trauma, it's natural, it is not attached to her and is not part of her identity.

The second suggests hope and understanding: the first, resignation and despair.

And the thing is, we all experience disordered thinking at one point. As experts would say, it's only when it becomes "life impacting" that it becomes an "illness". But isn't that a very abstract and fine line between a "feeling" and a "disorder"? Who are we letting decide what label society gives us? A label which will, whether we like it or not, determine a lot of our future.

By changing the narrative from the using the term "disorder" as a noun to an adjective, we could do a lot of good. The terms we mindlessly throw around (often, to be fair, in an attempt to normalise and open up the conversation about mental illness) are so important and powerful towards creating an image of mental health - yes, we should talk about it more, but we do need to be careful of the words we use.

Hearsay becomes general consensus. Let's be careful of what we let be heard.

The world can't ever be against you

For the longest time I would always say that the world was against me. Nothing seemed to go my way. But only now can I see how not only futile but how unhelpful this was. Because now, I have realised that, in the biggest and most important picture, there is no such thing as a good or bad thing. This idea was inspired by the amazing Eckhart Tolle in his 2009 publication.[3]

Look at it this way - has something "bad" ever happened to you or come into your life to cause a lot of angst and upset, but soon after, something very "good" comes out of it that wouldn't have happened had it not been for the "bad" thing? It's the butterfly effect - you never know if what course your life would take in the absence of one tiny event.

Can you ever say for sure that all the good in your life wouldn't have existed if there hadn't been some bad times too? Every event in the world is inextricably linked and cannot ever not be.

The reality is, there is order to everything in the world, a reason for every single event. But the problem is, our human consciousness can't comprehend it.

The world, right out to the cosmos, all has an order - there is no good or bad, no luck, and no mistakes, and the world can

---

[3] Tolle, E. (2009). A New Earth: The Life-Changing Follow Up to The Power of Now. 1st Edition. Penguin.

never be "against you". Those are all human constructs, created only because we will never be able to comprehend the true order of the universe.

But these human constructs, only creating limits, fear, anger and empty expectations, will always in the end be detrimental. The only true "bad" thing that can happen is caused by our human thoughts and perceptions.

Stop trying to control the world. Stop the black and white thinking - the labelling as things as good or bad for you. Of course, you can do things that improve your life, and you should never stop trying to, but the reality is, not everything will happen in your favour, and viewing it as "bad luck" or seeing that the world is against you won't ever help.

The best thing you can do is foster the phrase, "I don't mind." Try not to judge every event that happens - it's going to happen whichever way you choose to label it, so the best thing you can do - the only way that you can make something "good", as in not having a negative effect on you - is withdraw your black and white opinion.

The bottom line: accept the world as it comes and make the best of everything - it all happens under some sort of order. There is no such thing as good and bad.

Always hear what you need to

This is a big one. The next time someone tells you that you are being difficult, consider that it's just that they are finding it difficult to manipulate you.

Being someone who has naturally always wanted to please people, to give myself up for others, I have ended up facing lots of comments down the lines of "you're too sensitive", "you take everything too personally", or "you're being pathetic". And the more I realised my own worth, the more common this became. I used to take these to heart. But now, I can see that they only come when other people realise they can't control the situation.

You can never control how other people treat you. And even if you could, that would violate their own boundaries. What you can do though, is understand people and their thoughts enough to be able to hear or take what you need to from what they say or do to you. You're not pathetic, and you're not too sensitive - it's just that some people don't understand you and this frustrates them. But that's nothing on you. How other people treat you might be what they think of you (rightly or wrongly), but how you LET them treat you is what you think of YOURSELF.

It's vital that you don't internalise comments like these. Without going to deep and philosophical, there are so many theories that talk about self-concept development in terms of the idea of a "looking glass". Basically, we build our self-concept based on the way we think others perceive us. And this doesn't change even if we become super self-content and gun proof - the difference between someone with no self-worth and someone like this lies in the way they take how other people treat them. Understand that if anyone ever tells you that you are "too" something, it's usually just because they are struggling to make you act how THEY want you to.

Hear what you need to, hear what you know to be the real truth, and base your self-concept on the things that you know make you amazing.

What you think of yourself, you become

I've come a long way, but there are still things I'm working on. One of these is the massive difference in standards I have for myself and others.

If others have success, I'll massively inflate it and shower them with praise. If I have success, it's no big deal because I just expect it of myself. My self-standards are so disproportionately high that even the biggest achievements aren't praised.

And it's not only if I see success in others. If they struggle, it must just be because of things happening out with their control.

They need time and empathy. If *I* struggle, it must be my fault and what I need is to get over it and be better.

The result of this is that instinctively, without knowing anything about another person, I assume that they are better than me. But take this along with the way in which self-concept it developed on the previous page, and this becomes a vicious cycle:

1. You view others as better or more worthy,
2. You begin to live that out meaning you will subconsciously sit back and let success come to them and not you,
3. They pick up on this and start to treat you as less worthy,

4. You internalise that and begin to push yourself even lower down in your own self-perception.

The good thing is, I now know this to be learned behaviour. I now understand why I act like this. And the thing is, although ranking yourself against others is something we all do, it's something that is totally inconducive. (Ranking yourself above others is just as bad!) The key really is to focus on you and trust that you are where you are for a reason.

But this is just the first step - if you recognise this in yourself, you've taken it too. The next is to learn better behaviours, and this is what takes time and practise. I'm still working on this, but trust me, it's time and practise your future self with thank you for.

See yourself below others and you will subliminally act as though you are just that: trust that you're where you need to be, and you open the potential for growth and the progress that makes most sense to you.

When giving in is ok

In such a "progression" orientated culture - where careers are flying at super speed in so many paths, self-betterment and self-help is such a thing and information is available to everyone with ease - there has become so much pressure to always be moving towards goals and choosing a path and sticking to it. It is easy to understand why people are so afraid of falling off the wagon. "Giving in" has become a bit of a scare phrase. People are scared to look like a failure, to look weak, or to have to step back a little.

But you cannot ever control your surroundings, and it's inevitable then that things might go wrong. You might have a goal, but due to circumstances, it just becomes not possible. But in today's culture, a lot of people will feel they need to stick to it. And that's when anxiety or similar appears. You are trying to control things that are out of your control; it's a losing battle. But you've got to look "stoic" right? You can't be seen to give up. *Successful people never give up*.

Or maybe they do but you just don't see that part?

Much braver than the above, is to acknowledge your situation for what it is and let go of what you cannot control. Surrender to what you are trying to fight.

Don't get me wrong - high self-expectations and goals are important, but only if an acceptance of giving in when things aren't going well or when your gut tells you something is off comes in the same package. **Sometimes, giving in is ok.**

Choose your influences wisely

The people closest to you are your biggest influences. Choose them wisely. As much as we might want to think otherwise, deep down, how other people act towards you - the vibe they give you, how they talk to you, how they consider you, and how they treat you - is the very basis of how you form your self-image.

You can of course, control how you process and take their actions, but that takes time, and to be able to do that to the maximum takes years of self-awareness and regulation. Until then, any person making you feel anything other than person you want to become - or anyone encouraging and reinforcing negative self-talk - needs to either be removed from your life, or recognised for what they are.

It's cliche and often used without much meaning, but honestly, know your worth. These thoughts came about one day after time spent with my boyfriend when I was thinking about how genuinely happy I now am - how grateful I am for the people close to me today - and it made me realise that a while ago, I really didn't know my worth. (Well, I knew it, but I didn't act on it.) I made do to get by and continued to put others needs before mine.

Don't do this. Life is about so much more than just getting by. Know, and make choices, based on your worth. Nobody else can, or should, do it for you.

"Choose happy"

It's everywhere. But as much as, as discussed previously (see "Bad Days" and "Realistic Positivity"), it can be misconstrued (i.e., "just switch off your negative emotions and everything will be ok" which is very much not helpful) there's actually truth to it.

But the "choice" lies more in how you choose to view "happy" - whether you choose to achieve it through perspective or not.

Happiness isn't something that can be handed to you or instigated by a "thing". It's not materially determined, and there's a simple reason why: material things will always exist externally, and of such things, we have no control.

But what we do have control of is perspective, and that is how we can "choose" happy. Happiness comes from a perspective of gratitude (sometimes of material things, but also for things that aren't i.e., people, or connections). The material things might appear to make you happy but train yourself to be conscious of the WHY. If you buy a fancy pair of shoes, the shoes do not make you happy. What makes you happy is the gratitude in being able to afford something that you value. Practise this perspective.

A focus on material things fosters feelings of expectation (and hence disappointment) and a lack of control. You are depending on things coming to you to make you happy.

But a focus on gratitude brings certainty. You can never be disappointed if you focus on appreciating what you already have in front of you with every minute of each day, regardless of whether that's a materialistic thing or something else.

So how do you achieve this? Like I said above, it is practise. Never assume something external to you has made you "happy", but instead, train yourself to be able to view it as the fact that something **you** have done and controlled has brought that thing, person or relationship into your life.

For example, the gym isn't the thing that makes me happy. It's my gratitude for my body that allows me to progress every day. It's my appreciation for having a place to go so easily that lets me do this. It's the relationships that I have built with the amazing people there. I have control over all of those things, and realising that brings such a sense of calm and ease.

That's happiness.

The danger of confusing "self-love" with selfishness

I'm all for self-love. On realising just how much I used to self-sacrifice, I learnt the hard way just how important it is. But there's a point in which it can easily become selfishness, and while a lack of self-love is in-conducive mentally, so is the opposite. That is, if you lived a totally self-absorbed life, then you would be missing out on some basic needs.

As humans we are naturally social; we thrive on good connections, and it's natural to want to please others. But in a society where the narrative of "self-love first" is increasingly permeating our lives, we are increasingly encouraged not to do so. And in my opinion, that's going to lead to a lot of discontentment, and a sense in many of feeling like something is "missing".

With so much technology and things so readily available these days, people are becoming very independent. That is ok! But add to that this trend of almost forced self-love, and I think there is a risk of people totally isolating and going into themselves. Mentally, that's not ok.

In practising self-love, you ensure your own needs are met. Some say this is the key to happiness. I don't agree. Yes, you can't meet others needs if your own aren't met, but as always, there's a need for balance. Here's the difference:

Selfishness = only considering your own needs

Self-care = ensuring your own needs aren't always considered last

What I'm trying to say is don't feel like you are wrong or unhealthy if you naturally like to help others. Because of my past, I was doing this too much, and it was to my detriment. But at the same time, I've always naturally been a giver, and it's important to me that I don't lose this because of some bad experiences. I get a buzz from doing nice things for others, and that's ok. What it comes down to is self-awareness and the ability to recognise when you need to look after you first. Judge every different situation objectively, and not based on some blanket rule of "self-love first" that you feel like you need to live your life by.

Being kind and doing good for others breeds deep, satisfying connections. Self-love is of course needed but take it too far and these connections will start to suffer, and as a human, so will you!

Know this

You are never alone and never have been. I always knew this vaguely, but genuinely didn't have a clue of the extent of it until more recently.
I never quite believed that anyone else had it quite like me. Everyone else seemed to be doing so well despite any hardship people assured me they had.

The truth is, it would probably scare you how many people are in close to the exact same situation as you. You are NOT alone. You are not weird. You are not genetically faulty.

If every good day seems to be followed by a bad one, you're not alone.

If you think you're in a minority if you have a breakdown daily, you're not.

If you struggle with relationships, struggle to eat, struggle to stick to the gym, struggle to keep up a social life, struggle with drink, struggle to manage money, or struggle to raise your kids perfectly... you're just not alone.

As humans we strive to fit in, to feel part of something. That's part of the reason it can be so hard to be open in your struggles, whether with anxiety or anything else. But that's the paradox. There's no elite race of perfect humans that you should be aiming to be a part of. We all struggle - as little people with big feelings in a world that really, we don't have any control over, that's inevitable. The image of you sitting alone keeping all of all your worries to yourself whilst the rest of the world goes by can't possibly ever exist, so equally, it should never exist in your head. Anxiety lies!

The next time you're struggling, remember that, and no matter of how alone you feel, try to picture yourself amongst a **mass** of people who 100% "get" it. Because they **do** exist.

Forgiving yourself

How good are you at forgiving yourself?

I used to be awful at it. Not only does anxiety lend itself to feelings of guilt (as often anxiety arises in the first place due to something making you feel like you're not good enough) but having anxiety can also put you in a lot of situations where guilt is likely. For example, these were my guilt sources:

- My lack of contribution to my family due to not being able to work

- The stress and strain I put my friends and family under

- Giving up a place at music school when I became unwell and letting people down by going from straight A's to having to take time out of university

- The fact that I let anxiety consume me for so long and I couldn't just "snap out of it" (the biggest one)

Seeing old pictures of myself - of times when I was struggling the most - used to really trigger me. I couldn't look at them without floods of negative emotions. But not anymore.

Although anxiety has caused me so much pain, it was also literally there to protect me. I did what I had to at the time to get by, and for that, I should be grateful for myself. It was there to tell me something, and at the end of the day, coming through it, I have gained such a deeper understanding of life and myself. It wasn't anything external that got me through it - it was me, my body and my mind. Similarly, there's absolutely nothing to say that every one of those bad experiences didn't play a part in shaping who I am today. Although life landed me in some horrible situations in the past, it was the same body that got me through them as the one that I am in today.

Sure, if things had been different, some suffering could have been avoided. But if things had been different there's nothing to say something else bad wouldn't have happened.

So whatever struggle you've found yourself in, then or now, forgive yourself. Your body only ever does what it does to protect you. Don't see your experiences as what your mind has done TO you, but what it has done FOR you.

Tell yourself why you are grateful for you today, as in reality, it's you who has gotten you through every painful situation you've ever been in.

What you've done is who you are, but what you do now is what you will be.

Anxiety puts you beneath nobody

Everyone has flaws: some people are horribly messy; some have anger issues; some people can be self-centred. But none of these really get in the way of adulthood.

And some people, for whatever reason, end up suffering anxious tendencies. And as many of you will know, the effects this can have on careers, social lives and relationships can be drastic. But does that make these people any lesser?

The answer, of course, is no. The problem is, in our society, the tendencies of people with anxiety - so much more so than other character flaws mentioned - are very incompatible with what it takes to become "successful" in our modern world.

For example, to take the person whose flaws include self-centeredness, the reality is that these people will probably do well career wise, especially in today's out-for-yourself Capitalist business world. They will probably then have good social lives and opportunities (from the outside anyway). But take the person with anxiety, and there's a higher likelihood that they won't be able to hold down a job or maintain a relationship. But does this make their flaws any worse?

To the person with anxiety, looking out at that person who is good at "adulting", regardless of how nice of a person they are, then yes, the answer is yes. But this isn't true.

Despite what our society might make it look like, just because one of your flaws is anxiety, it does not make it ANY less of a person than anyone else. Because everyone has flaws, it's just that 21st century life seems to accommodate some of these more than others. That's the harsh reality. But which person would you rather be?

For me, the key is to realise that, if you are prone to anxiety, the truth is that this makes you able to experience life at a deeper level. It might be making life harder today, but embrace that, and transcend it in the knowledge that one day, that deeper level will make you able to experience life with so much more meaning and fulfilment. Although society makes it seem so, the obvious indicators of being good at "adulting" are not the only measures of prosperity. Accept that and commit to working towards what success means for you, and one day, you will no longer feel "beneath" **anyone.**

Happy or content?

Are you happy or content? Which would you rather be?

Being happy is a clearly a good thing, but as you have read, it's also true to say that this obsessive focus on positivity could be turning a little toxic. In our culture it has, in some ways, become a bit of a pressure to always be happy, and as I said previously, this isn't sustainable or realistic. This got me thinking about the difference between happiness and contentment (yes, there's a difference).

Happiness is a momentary mood or feeling. It's largely dependent on external factors and how they are affecting you in the current moment. Yes, it can come from within you, but it's also impossible to ensure that the current moment and state of affairs won't change your mood at the flip of a coin.

Contentment, though, is generally a longer-term state that is more intrinsically focused and influenced. It's a feeling of fulfilment, satisfaction and purpose in life, which is increased by anything which moves you to your own personal goals and ambitions.

Hopefully you see the difference from my explanation, because the next bit is important! Depending on whether you focus on happiness or contentment, you will view and be able to accept "bad days", or any feelings other than "happiness" differently.

Focus on happiness, and you will be disheartened by bad days or sadness. Because it's more externally orientated and influenced, you'll feel a pressure to always feel and appear happy, and ironically, this will make you feel the very opposite if you can't live up it (or rather when you can't live up to it - remember you can never control external factors).

BUT focus on contentment, and you realise that the gradation of individual days isn't as relevant. More relevant is the overarching direction you are taking your life in and the satisfaction, gratitude and fulfilment which comes as a result. That's what brings true peace and acceptance in yourself. It doesn't matter about the "good vibes" you give to the world - it matters how deeply you are looking in to, and listening to, yourself to ensure that your life is going the way you want.

Unpopular opinion - a constant state of mindfulness isn't possible

True mindfulness means being present in the moment and accepting of what is without any focus on worries, stresses or over-analyses' of life.

But as I have explained before, it's never possible to switch off your "negative radio station". It's part of being human.

The more you aim for this state of constant mindfulness and resist natural and inevitable self-doubt, worries and stresses, the more you lessen your capacity for true times of mindfulness.

As Russ Harris again wrote, it's like riding a bike[4]. You are always going side to side and avoiding falling off. The better you get at riding a bike though - the better you get at engaging in true, non-judgemental and accepting mindfulness to avoid the pull of inevitable unhelpful thinking - the better you become at it. But the occasional swaying or the occasional distraction from the here and now by your thinking self (the voices you can never switch off) will never cease.

---

[4] Harris, R. (2008). *The Happiness Trap: Stop Struggling, Start Living.* Robinson Publishing.

Resistance will always be there. It gets easier to control, but it doesn't go away. And that's ok. You're human - stop avoiding difficulty.

As they say, through suffering comes opportunity for growth.

Anxiety in times of stress

I'm writing this book in 2020. I'm sure you can see where the need for these thoughts came from. But they don't only apply to living during a global pandemic - they can apply to any times of extreme upheaval or stress.

During such times, we can't expect ourselves to be 100% every day and that's ok. But we can definitely do things to help ourselves. Here are my top tips for reducing anxiety during times of hardship:

1. **Have a go-to-thought that you can focus all of your energy in to whenever you notice anxious or negative thoughts begin to creep in**.

This is something I have come to do habitually - I never used to be able to do it and you might not be able to at first, but with practise I promise you will get better, and it honestly is the most helpful thing I have found to do. Whenever you feel yourself begin to become fixed on a spiral of negative or worrying thoughts, STOP whatever you are doing and put ALL of your energy in to picturing and imagining a happy event. For example, I often think about future holidays, my dog, or big events with my boyfriend. Immerse yourself in the thought and sit there until the negative thoughts aren't as intrusive.

2. **Make a conscious effort to have conversations with people close to you about something totally unrelated to whatever is causing stress in your life every day.**

Talk about music, sports, work, your pets - *anything*, as long as it is not related to whatever the root of the upset in your life. You will, of course, at times feel the need to discuss what's going on, and that's healthy, but be sure to set aside times when you don't.

3. **Do one activity each day that you enjoy or that satisfies you**.

When something stressful is going on in your life, it can be easy to let it get in the way of everything, but being rational, it doesn't need to. It doesn't have to affect reading, being creative, listening to music, playing video games, educating yourself on something you've always wanted to know about, walking, or baking to (name a just few). Don't feel guilty for spending time on you, even if it's just chilling with a movie - five years down the line all that will matter is that you got through the stressful time. Some people will deal with such situations by being super productive but that does *not* mean you have to too.

I'm doing lots of "happy activities" but I'm still not happy?

"Get your head in to work"
"Do a good workout"
"Start a new hobby"
"Go a big walk"
"Give to others or charity"
"Go out with friends"

Any of these sound familiar? Being activities commonly recommended as things to do to improve happiness, I have heard my fair share of these. They may provide some short-term relief, sure.

But a lot of the time, you will probably find that after a while, the extent to which they can make you feel "happier" decreases. Whether or not this happens will depend on your intentions on beginning the activity. This will determine whether they become:

a) Value-guided actions, or
b) Control strategies

A value guided action is an activity which is done because it is meaningful to you, brings you enjoyment, and adds value to your life. It brings satisfaction and fulfilment.

A control strategy though, is an activity done in the pursuit of distraction from some inner conflict or distress. By the time your brain has committed energy in to keeping focus on the fun task at hand, there is none left to actually feel satisfaction or true enjoyment. It's a bit like putting a little plaster on a serious wound.

Control strategies, of course, do have their place in terms of providing short term relief or a temporary escape from some trauma that your brain isn't yet able to process. But if not accompanied by time committed to working through and addressing inner conflict and issues, they will only lead to more frustration and despair as your brain comes to associate once-fun activities with stress and upset.

Things like long walks outdoors or smashing a workout will do wonders for your real-time headspace and will help in the process of overcoming mental struggle, but only if they are combined with attempts to resolve what is actually causing the distress in the first place will you truly flourish.

Procrastination and fear of change

What is the biggest thing stopping you from making the changes you really want in life? For many, the reason will be fear of change. Procrastination, at a deep level, is primarily a protective mechanism. It's called the "comfort of discomfort" - it's much more comfortable to sit where you are, regardless of how happy you are, than to initiate change.

What if it goes wrong? What if the risk doesn't pay off? These fears make it the easiest thing in the world to always put things off until "tomorrow" (or rather, some abstract point in the future). But the reality is, that fear will still be there tomorrow.

But if, when you were, say, two years old, you were scared of change and always put off progressing yourself until tomorrow, where would you be now? I know I wouldn't like to be stuck at that stage.

The ironic thing is though, that it's the development of an intelligent adult mind that stops us from growing without fear as we did as children. Humans are programmed for constant growth. Non sentient animals are a little different - a baby giraffe will be walking pretty instantly after it's born and within a few weeks will have learned most of what it ever will to become independent. Humans are very much the opposite - our brains are still developing until 25, and even then, the fully developed brain is hugely capable of change. There seems to be an idea that it is kids who learn and develop, but as adults, we should find our calling then sustain it. And that's where procrastination fuelled by fear of change comes from.

But the reality is, if you know deep down that you want more, you will never be content.

Instead of letting your adult brain convince you then, that it's better for you to be comfortable in that familiar discomfort, use it to overcome that instinct to procrastinate. Get excited about the changes you can make. Notice the hype you feel when you get the ball rolling, and the motivation that comes with it. Acknowledge how good you feel every step of the way, not just when you reach that final goal.

Because change and growth is amazing. It's what we were made for. You love it - it is your ego that doesn't, and luckily, you're inconceivably stronger than that.

Why NOW is a good time

Whatever your goals or dreams are, it is easy to convince yourself that whatever it is you want to achieve is unachievable: that you've left it too late; that you can't commit enough time or energy to making that change. As you now know however, that is your ego talking. The familiar is comfortable, and the unfamiliar, new and different you, is uncomfortable. It takes energy, it takes time, and it might take some compromise to achieve it. But the ego is not you. Your gut feeling is you - that gut feeling that always sneaks in and gets you thinking about a future you that you would really love to be.

Take me. I recently qualified as a primary teacher. On leaving university I was urged to apply for PhD scholarships. I love working with children and I definitely have a passion to go back to university and study further. But with a lot going on in my life last year on top of all the obvious, and my head not really being in it, I knew that it didn't feel right. What felt right was working out, strengthening my body and mind, and the prospect of helping others to do the same. That's why I changed route.

Parts of me (my ego) told me it was too late to qualify as a Personal Trainer. I had chosen my path as a teacher and that was that. But after speaking to some amazing people, I realised that of course this wasn't true. So at the start of lockdown in 2020, I began studying and became a Personal Trainer. I know I want to do a PhD one day, but right now, personal training is what feels right.

If you want something enough, now is always the right time. Listen to your gut. You are not "too old", and it's not "too late".

Say you're 24 right now. You have a dream to study to become a nurse. Say it takes 4 years. Your ego will tell you that nobody qualifies at 28. Nobody starts a career at 28.

But whether or not you take the leap to chase your dream, in four years' time, you are still going to be 28. The difference being that one 28-year-old will still be wishing they are something they aren't, and one will have just become that.

It's not too late. You do have the time. If you want something enough, now is always the right time, because you can make it so, and you owe that to yourself. Listen to that gut - it knows.

Strength comes from struggle - anxiety and the gym

Both mentally and physically.

The strength of both aspects are undeniably linked. For me, as I mentioned at the beginning of this book, when I was faced with the task of overcoming adversity in both, it was definitely my (conscious) focus on physical strength that kick started my recovery, and that's because, to me, mental strength is a by-product of physical.

And that's key. Mental health is such a massively hard thing to think about, talk about, track and monitor, and that's because it's so abstract. You, and only you, knows where you are at mentally, and even then, half the time your subconscious is running the place without your knowledge or understanding. As you have read, this makes it hard to believe that you'll ever get better - hard to map a way out and see the light at the end of the tunnel.

But physical strength and growth is a little different. Changes are so much easier to notice and celebrate; small goals and steps seem much more tangible. Physical growth to me is a much more uniform process, and not only that, but you can much more easily enrol the help of others in your journey.

And as I've said before, once my body physically started to overcome trauma, it's as if it showed my brain that mentally it can do the exact same - and it did. The gym 100% made me both realise and refine my mental strength despite my past. I really believe that with physical strength comes better mental health and resilience.

That's why if you are reading this book, I can't recommend physical exercise enough. It absolutely got me out of a hole mentally and I know it can do the same for everyone else.

Progressive strength of body teaches your brain of its capability to build strength of mind in the face of adversity.

You can train your mind just like you train your body. Believing in this can be hard, but by starting with the obvious of strengthening your body physically, your body will learn just what it is capable of mentally.

After all, as I once failed to see, it's the exact same brain that directs and controls both processes.

I hope more than anything that reading this book has brought you some hope and helped you on your way to overcoming anxiety. If I can be of any further help at all, please do not hesitate to get in touch with me in one of the following ways:

Email: sophie.cathcart@googlemail.com

Instagram: @skc.pt

Some writing that has inspired my mental journey

Brass, J. (2019). *Own Your Anxiety: 99 Simple Ways to Channel Your Secret Edge.* Page Two Publishing.

Harris, R. (2008). *The Happiness Trap: Stop Struggling, Start Living.* Robinson Publishing.

Krishnamurti, J. (2018). *What Are You Doing With Your Life?* Rider Publishing.

Paul, S. (2019). *The Wisdom of Anxiety: How worry and intrusive thoughts are gifts.* Aster Publishing.

Peters, S. (2012). *The Chimp Paradox: The Mind Management Programme to Help You Achieve Success, Confidence and Happiness: The Acclaimed Mind Management Programme to Help You Achieve Success, Confidence and Happiness.* 1st Edition. Vermilion Publishing.

Tolle, E. (2001). *The Power of Now: A Guide to Spiritual Enlightenment.* 20th Anniversary Edition. Hodder and Stoughton Publishing.

Tolle, E. (2009). *A New Earth: The Life-Changing Follow Up to The Power of Now.* 1st Edition. Penguin Publishing.

Printed in Great Britain
by Amazon